2x 4/15 LT 3/13

Xtreme Athletes

Michelle Wie

Michelle Wie

Jeff C. Young

MORGAN
REYNOLDS
PUBLISHING

Greensboro, North Carolina

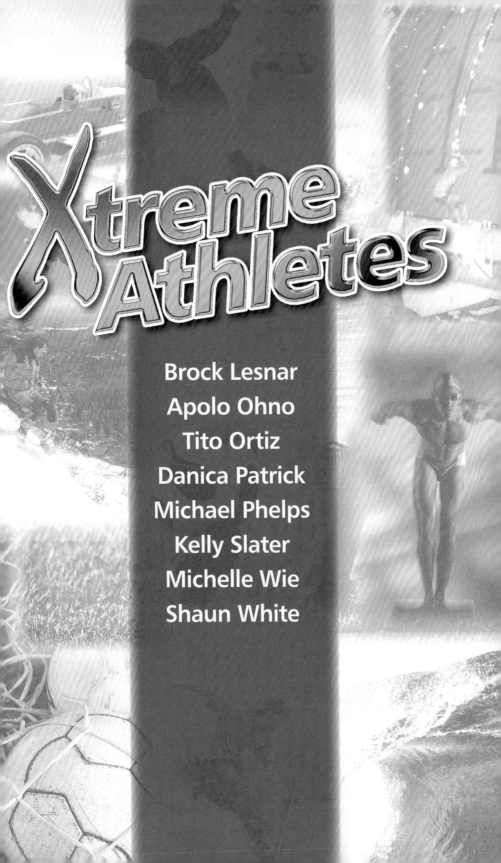

Xtreme Athletes

Brock Lesnar
Apolo Ohno
Tito Ortiz
Danica Patrick
Michael Phelps
Kelly Slater
Michelle Wie
Shaun White

Xtreme Athletes: Michelle Wie

Copyright © 2012 by Morgan Reynolds Publishing

Library of Congress Cataloging-in-Publication Data

Young, Jeff C., 1948-
 Xtreme athletes : Michelle Wie / by Jeff C. Young.
    p. cm.
 Includes bibliographical references and index.
  ISBN 978-1-59935-187-2 -- ISBN 978-1-59935-212-1 (e-book) 1. Wie,
Michelle--Juvenile literature. 2. Golfers--United
States--Biography--Juvenile literature. 3. Women golfers--United
States--Biography--Juvenile literature. I. Title. II. Title: MIchelle Wie.
 GV964.W49Y68 2012
 796.352082--dc23

                                        2011020799

Printed in the United States of America
First Edition

To my longtime Hoosier friends,
Richard K. and Angela Roark Jones

Michelle Wie

Contents

Michelle driving off at
the sixth hole at the
Weetabix Women's
British Open in July 2005

one
Little Girl, Big Swing

Michelle Wie's body language said it all. After tapping in her final putt to win her first professional individual tournament in 2009, she gleefully retrieved her ball, looked to the sky, sighed deeply, and jumped up and down while pumping her right fist. "Wowwwww . . . . . . ," Michelle posted on her Twitter account, "never thought this would feel THIS great!!!!"

Michelle had played in sixty-five Ladies Professional Golf Association (LPGA) Tour events, and finally she had proven her doubters and detractors wrong. For any other twenty-year-old pro golfer, winning their first pro event would have been heralded as a great beginning instead of an "it's about time" milestone. But when you play in your first LPGA Tour event when you're only twelve, you're expected to win soon and win often. And when you unabashedly say that you want to compete with the men on the Professional Golf Association (PGA) Tour, that increases the expectations even more.

Michelle Sung Wie was born in Honolulu, Hawaii, on October 11, 1989. Her parents named her after a song by the Beatles. Both of her parents were born

in South Korea and were skilled golfers. Her father, Byung-Wook (B. J.), is an avid 2-handicap golfer. Her mother, Kyung-Hee (Bo), was South Korea's women's amateur golf champion in 1985.

When Michelle was born, her father was working as a professor in the School of Travel Industry

Honolulu, Hawaii

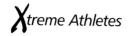

Management at the University of Hawaii at Manoa. The Wies played in a local golf league at the Olomana Golf Links in Hawaii. Michelle would tag along when her parents played. One day, B. J. took his four-year-old daughter to a vacant baseball diamond to let her tee off on a golf ball. He gave her a sawed off club to swing.

She imitated the stance she had seen her parents use and eyed the small white ball by her feet. She swung as hard as she could and watched the ball soar into the air, bounce, and roll. Then, she looked at her father to let him know she wanted to try it again. From that moment on, golf began to define Michelle's life. When she wasn't practicing, she was watching PGA and LPGA Tour events on television. She preferred the PGA Tour events because the men could hit the ball longer and harder. She decorated her bedroom with a poster of Tiger Woods. Her parents encouraged her. They never made Michelle feel that a career as a pro golfer was just a silly, childish dream that would never come true.

When she was seven, her parents took her to a local municipal course. The man in charge asked Michelle how old she was. After she told him she was seven, he said, "Sorry, Too young." Even then, Michelle felt that talent was more important than age. "What I really wanted to tell him was, 'I can beat you!'"

He thought that he might humble Michelle by pairing her up with an adult. Michelle surprised her opponent by outdistancing her on drives and shooting a 1-under 2 on a 200-yard, par 3 hole. After playing nine holes, Michelle's partner walked off the course.

By age nine, Michelle was regularly beating her parents. They may have felt like they had nothing left to teach her. They went looking for someone to mentor their daughter. That's when Casey Nakama, the head pro at the Olomana Golf Links, became Michelle's first golf coach.

Although he hadn't played in any PGA events, Nakama had experience playing in the less lucrative Asian Tour and the Hogan Tour in the United States. But he gave it up for the financial security of being a club pro. When he first saw Michelle play, he saw a lot of potential and raw talent, but he also spotted a lot of flaws in her game. What impressed him the most was her size. At age ten, Michelle was already over five feet tall. "She could carry the ball 200 yards," Nakama recalled. "But the only thing she had going for her was her size. Her swing plane was flat and laid-off. Her short game was really bad. She didn't know what she was doing."

Nakama would soon find that Michelle also had a keen intelligence and an exceptional work ethic that would set her apart from many other young golfers. Michelle began reading shortly after her first birthday.

She was also bilingual, since her parents spoke to her in both Korean and English.

"What was really unusual about her was that she was so driven at what she did," Nakama said. "Even at 10 years old, she didn't mind practicing every day. She was just determined to do whatever we were working on. We would make a swing adjustment, and she would work on it and come back in three or four days and say, 'I think that I've got it Casey.' That work ethic, it separates her from a lot of the other players."

In 2000, Michelle won the girl's division of the Oahu Junior Championship. A year later, she won both the Hawaii State Women's Stroke Championship and the Jennie K. Wilson Women's Invitational. The latter event was considered to be the most prestigious women's amateur tournament in Hawaii. Nakama found that competition made Michelle even more focused and intense about her game. "Competing made her even more driven," Nakama said. "Even at eleven years old, she got really intense."

Already, the local media was taking notice of Michelle. On June 30, 2000, the *Honolulu Star-Advertiser* reported that Michelle had become the youngest player to qualify for the Women's Amateur Public Links. A writer for the Associated Press asked Michelle how it felt to be playing against adults and older girls. Her answer showed a maturity and seriousness that belied her age. "I just think about my

Michelle at age eleven with her mother, Kyung-Hee (Bo) Wie, at the Olomana Golf Course in Honolulu

game," Michelle said. "I don't really think about other people."

Soon, news about Michelle's golfing achievements had spread well beyond Hawaii. In the fall of 2000, employees of Jay Leno contacted the Wies and invited Michelle to appear as a guest on *The Tonight Show.* Her parents declined the offer. Michelle was about to start a new school year at a new school, and the show would have been too much of a distraction.

Michelle's new school, The Punahou School, had a well-earned reputation as one of America's best private schools. President Barack Obama and America Online co-founder Steve Case are two of the school's best known alumni. Since her father was a university professor, he knew and emphasized the importance of a good education. According to the school's Web site, the class of 2010 had a median GPA of 3.47 on a 4-point scale. Typically, the school has 2,300 applicants for five hundred openings.

But once Michelle got acclimated to her new school environment, her father had her playing against a higher level of competition–adult men. Michelle had pretty much run out of female competition in Hawaii. There were only two or three annual women's tournaments in Hawaii. Naturally, there was resentment and resistance from both men and women golfers. Nakama even warned Michelle's father about it. "Whether you know or not," he told B. J., "you're insulting the women on the LPGA."

Michelle's first competition against men was at the ninety-third Manoa Cup Hawaii State Amateur Match-Play Championship in Honolulu. The Manoa Cup is Hawaii's oldest continuous golf tournament. At the age of eleven, Michelle became the first female and the youngest golfer to compete in that tournament.

In a match play event, golfers are paired off and they play against each other instead of the whole field.

The golfer with the lowest score on the most holes is the winner. Sometimes, it's not necessary to play all eighteen holes. If a golfer has a 10 to 6 lead after sixteen holes, they skip the last two holes. It's even possible for a match to end after playing only ten holes.

In 2001, Michelle was eliminated in the first round, but a year later she came back to become the first female and the youngest golfer to advance to the second round. In the second round, she lost an extra-holes playoff to Del-Muc Fujita by one stroke. Fujita told a writer from *Golf for Women* magazine that he felt lucky to win. "I was very lucky to win," Fujita said. "She had me down three strokes after nine holes. I mean her shot trajectory and strength are amazing. I literally had to force myself to quit watching her swing. I looked at the sky instead. She was driving as far as I was on most holes; she was already, like, six inches taller than me; and pretty soon I was thinking, 'What advantage do I really have here?' "

It was becoming more commonplace to hear Michelle's name and "the youngest to" or "the youngest female golfer to" in the same sentence. In February 2002, it was being heard again when Michelle qualified for her first LPGA event. At that time, she was a few months away from completing the seventh grade.

Michelle got in by becoming a Monday qualifier. A Monday qualifier is an amateur golfer with a handicap of 3.4 strokes or less. On the Monday before

A view of Mauna Kea Resort, one
of the top golf courses in Hawaii

the tournament starts, the potential Monday qualifiers play one round. The two golfers with the lowest scores are then allowed to compete in the tournament.

The tournament was the Takefuji Classic, and it was held on a Hawaiian course that Michelle was familiar with. In her Monday qualifying round, Michelle shot an unimpressive 83, but she was playing in some adverse conditions. There were thirty-mile an-hour winds and rain. When the tournament started, the winds died down, and Michelle shot an even-par 72 in the first round.

In the second round, Michelle shot a 2-over 74, and she failed to advance in the tournament. That's known as missing the cut. After two rounds the bottom half of the field is eliminated. Still, it gave Michelle a taste of what it was like to compete against the best women golfers in the world. After missing the cut, she told some reporters how she felt and what she had learned. "I had lots of fun, but it was tougher than I thought," Michelle said. "Maybe because I was thinking more than I should. The competition here is way different. They're more consistent and you have to be on the fairway. Every shot counts."

The same month that Michelle competed in her first LPGA event, she met Gary Gilchrist. Gilchrist had heard about Michelle while he was teaching at the David Leadbetter Golf Academy in

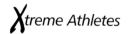

Bradenton, Florida. He traveled to Hawaii to get a firsthand look at this young girl who had created such a stir. During lunch, Michelle told Gilchrist that her goal was to play on both the LPGA and the PGA Tours. He was impressed with her ambition, but he was understandably skeptical. "That's great," he told Michelle, "but do you have what it takes?"

After lunch, Michelle gave him a display of her raw talent. They went to a nearby driving range. Along with Gilchrist, there were about a dozen onlookers. Some of them had seen Michelle hit drives before. Unlike Gilchrist, they knew what to expect.

As Michelle teed the ball, Gilchrist looked for some sign of nervousness or anxiety from her. She looked perfectly calm and composed. Her first drive left him awestruck. Michelle unleashed a powerful and fluid swing that sent the ball soaring past the 230-yard marker. "I had never seen any boy her age swing a club like that, much less a girl," Gilchrist recalled. "The control. The fluidity. The power. And it was all natural."

Michelle proceeded to show Gilchrist that her first drive wasn't a fluke. She continued to crush drive after drive. He was astonished to watch a young girl drive the ball so far while making it look so effortless. His only reservation about Michelle was her desire to excel and dominate. "I don't think that winning was everything to Michelle," Gilchrist said. "She just loved hitting the ball."

Gilchrist was sold on Michelle. But now, he had to sell her parents on the idea of leaving Hawaii so Michelle could become his star pupil at the Leadbetter Academy.

THE LPGA

The Ladies Professional Golf Association (LPGA) was founded in 1950 by a group of thirteen professional women golfers. Today, it's the oldest ongoing women's professional sports organization in the United States. Based in Daytona Beach, Florida, the organization is best known for running the LPGA Tour. The annual tour features the world's best women golfers in a series of weekly tournaments that run from February to December.

Before the LPGA was founded, the Women's

Professional Golfers Association (WPGA) sponsored three open championships which allowed the best women golfers to compete for prize money. But the organization was never able to attract any wealthy financial backers or corporate sponsors. The WPGA was also unable to affiliate itself with the well established PGA.

In its early years, the organization grew slowly but steadily. By 1952, it had a schedule of twenty-one events and by 1959, the LPGA Tour prize money increased to $200,000. Still, it was very difficult for a woman to make a living as a pro golfer in those days. The players on the LPGA Tour would often carpool to events and pitch in to share expenses. Between events, they would pick up some extra income by giving exhibitions and clinics.

The emergence of Mickey Wright as the premier woman's golfer in the late 1950s and early 1960s heightened interest in and media coverage of the LPGA Tour. Between 1959 and 1968, Wright averaged around eight tour wins a year. For five consecutive years (1960-1964), Wright won the Vare Trophy for the lowest scoring average on the LPGA Tour. Her engaging manner and superb golfing skills won over golf writers who had been reluctant to cover women's golf.

One of Wright's LPGA contemporaries noted, "Mickey got the outside world to take a second look at women golfers and when they looked they discovered the rest of us."

Another LPGA Tour player the media discovered around that time was Kathy Whitworth. From 1962 to 1985, Whitworth won a record eighty-eight LPGA Tour events. Since no PGA or LPGA golfer has won more events, that makes Whitworth the winningest professional golfer of all time. Whitworth was also named the LPGA's Player of the Year seven times.

In the late 1970s, Nancy Lopez emerged as one of the LPGA Tour's most dominating players. In 1978, Lopez set a record by winning nine tournaments in one calendar year. The following year, she won another eight tournaments. Before retiring in 1987, Lopez had won the Vare Trophy three times and the LPGA's Player of the Year Award four times.

The 1980s and 1990s were marked by escalating prize money and media coverage. In 1979, the annual prize money total for the LPGA Tour was $4.4 million. By 1989 it had more than tripled to a sum of $14 million. By 1996, it had climbed to $25.3 million.

During the early years of the twenty-first century, the LPGA has had an influx of players born outside of the USA. In 2009, 122 non-Americans from twenty-seven countries were competing on the LPGA Tour. From 2001 to 2010 the LPGA's Player of the Year has gone to a golfer born outside of America. Sweden-born Annika Sorenstam won the award five consecutive years (2001-2005). Her streak was ended by Mexican native, Lorena Ochoa, who went on to win it four years in a row (2006-2009). Ochoa's streak was ended by Yani Tseng who was born in Taiwan.

Some golf writers think that the biggest problem currently facing the LPGA is a lack of television coverage from one of the major networks. In 2011, only one of the LPGA Tour's four major tournaments (the Kraft Nabisco Championship) was scheduled to receive televised coverage. That event was aired on the Golf Channel which is a cable network. LPGA golfer Angela Sanford told the *Palm Beach Post* that a dominant player emerging on the LPGA Tour could really increase fan interest. "We need one player. It would help if it was an American . . . to win six or eight tournaments a year, one of them being a major; someone who is right there every week and dominates; someone to pound it at them and just keep winning."

Maybe Michelle Wie will still become that player. ∎

Thirteen-year-old Michelle poses with the championship cup after winning the 2003 USGA Women's Amateur Public Links Championship at Ocean Hammock Golf Club in Palm Coast, Florida.

two

A Teenage Phenom

Gilchrist approached Michelle's parents with what he thought was a very tempting offer—a full scholarship to the Leadbetter Academy. Michelle would get free room and board and all the training and instruction to help her realize her vast potential.

Her parents rejected the offer. At that time, they had no interest in leaving Hawaii. B. J. had a secure position as a university professor. Bo was well established and doing well as a realtor in Honolulu. They were also satisfied that Michelle was getting an excellent education at the prestigious Punahou School.

Gilchrist knew that they weren't going to change their minds, so he offered them a compromise. Michelle would come to the Leadbetter Academy for lessons and instructions when she was on break from the Punahou School. "They loved Hawaii, so I didn't

try and sell them on moving to Bradenton," Gilchrist said. "I sold them on coming there and taking lessons from me and helping improve her there."

The Wies began making enough trips to rack up frequent flier miles. Much has been written about how Michelle's parents were always hovering around her at practices and competitions. Another coach might have been irked by their behavior, but Gilchrist saw it as a positive influence. "Being around her parents, she was very mature," Gilchrist noted. "She thought very logically, like her parents."

The family decision to take on a new coach created some hard feelings. Casey Nakama learned about Michelle's meeting with Gilchrist by reading about it in the newspaper. He had known that sooner or later, Michelle would move on to another coach and someplace that offered better facilities than Olomana. Nakama thought that Michelle's father would call him to let him know, but, he didn't hear from B. J., so he requested to talk to him privately.

That's when he learned that his services were no longer needed. Nakama accepted that, but he wondered where Michelle would practice when she was in Hawaii. He assumed that the people at Olomana wouldn't let her practice for free. He went to the club owner to ask about Michelle receiving complimentary access to the facility. Nakama then learned that B. J. had already met with the club owner to ask for permission for Michelle to play there for free. "He didn't have to go behind my back," Nakama said. "If he had any balls, he'd have told me not to bother. It would have been fine. But he slides around."

Gilchrist also had an uncomfortable parting of the ways. He had been coaching Paula Creamer. Like Michelle, Creamer was a young golfer with tremendous potential. As an amateur, Creamer would win nineteen national titles. Since joining the LPGA Tour in 2005, she's won nine LPGA Tour events including the U.S. Women's Open in 2010.

Since the Wies wanted him as Michelle's full-time coach, Gilchrist had to let Paula and her parents know that he was leaving their employ to coach a younger golfer. "Paula felt like I betrayed her," Gilchrist said.

Once Gilchrist became Michelle's full-time coach, he worked at improving all aspects of her game— putting, chipping, and hitting the ball with accuracy and learning all the different types of shots. Michelle had an aversion to running, so Gilchrist got her to ride a stationary bike. "My philosophy is to work on the technical part, then on feel," Gilchrist explained. "Then I would challenge her in competition so she could take what she learned to the golf course. We worked on every area, different shots, chipping out of thick rough, flop shots. You had to keep her challenged all the time or she would lose interest."

The lessons that Michelle was learning were improving both her game and her confidence. In 2002, Michelle played in the Women's Hawaiian State Open, instead of the Junior Division. She easily won the event by shooting an 8-under par and finishing 13 strokes ahead of her nearest competitor. The best women golfers in Hawaii had been routed by a twelve-year-old girl.

Michelle's impressive victory in the Hawaiian State Open led to an invitation to compete in the 2003 Kraft Nabisco Championship. The event had a history of allowing amateurs to compete against the pros on the LPGA Tour. With the interest she was generating in women's golf, Michelle was a logical choice. Most amateurs who competed, played two rounds, missed the cut, and then went back home.

Michelle was paired in the first round with two other young golfers who would later become stars on the LPGA Tour—Natalie Gulbis and Christine Kim. In the third round, Michelle shot a 66. That showed everyone that she could compete with the seasoned pros on the LPGA Tour. She finished in a tie for ninth place. At the age of thirteen, she became the youngest player to make the cut in an LPGA event. The only negative was that Michelle

Michelle listens to her father and caddie, B. J. Wie, while they try to decide on the proper club at the fifth hole during the opening round of the 2003 Kraft Nabisco Championship in Rancho Mirage, California.

wasn't allowed to keep the $35,000 in prize money that she had won. At that time, she was still an amateur.

The next big event for Michelle was the U.S. Women's Amateur Public Links Championship. It's a unique competition sponsored by the United States Golf Association (USGA). The event is open only to female amateurs who play on public golf courses. Country Club members are not allowed to compete.

The event has three stages. Every golfer attempting to enter the event has to win a spot by going through several days of qualifying play. The qualifying play reduces the field to 128 golfers. The second stage is two days of what's known as stroke play. The sixty-four golfers with the lowest number of strokes for thirty-six holes move on to the final stage, and the other sixty-four are eliminated from the field. The final stage is match play between two players. The match play continues until only two are left. Then, the finalists have a thirty-six-hole playoff to determine the winner.

Michelle reached the championship round by winning five consecutive matches. Her opponent in the championship round was a twenty-one-year-old amateur named Virada Nirapathpongporn from Thailand. She was a very formidable opponent. In 2002, she had won the NCAA women's individual championship while playing for Duke University.

Michelle got off to a slow start. After eight holes, she was four behind Nirapathpongporn. But she battled back. They were tied after eighteen holes. Nirapathpongporn and Michelle continued their heated back and forth match well into the second round. After thirty-four holes, they were still tied.

Michelle was able to take the lead on the thirty-fifth hole. She made par and Nirapathpongporn surprisingly missed a three-foot putt. That put Michelle one up. Both golfers made par on the final hole. A thirteen-year-old girl had defeated a twenty-one-year old national college champion. The youngest player to make a cut in an LPGA event now was also the youngest player to win a USGA event.

To put Michelle's win in perspective, it's been pointed out that Tiger Woods was fifteen when he won his first national championship. Jack Nicklaus was seventeen. Among women golfers, Mickey Wright was seventeen and Nancy Lopez was fifteen when they won their first national championship.

In the weeks following her latest win, Michelle was contacted by television networks, ABC, NBC, CNN, BBC, and ESPN. There were also calls from such television shows as *Today*, *60 Minutes*, *David Letterman* and *The Tonight Show with Jay Leno*. Numerous other media outlets were clamoring to interview Michelle. Major newspapers in the U.S. and in Asia were writing stories about a teenaged

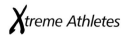
sensation who had revitalized interest in women's golf.

Michelle was trying to deal with all that attention while getting caught up on school work and reconnecting with her friends. She only had a few weeks of rest before trying to qualify for the biggest event in women's golf—the U.S. Women's Open.

While Michelle was able to qualify for the prestigious U.S. Women's Open, her performance there would lead to criticism and controversy. Some of the sharpest criticism and cutting remarks would be directed at her father, B. J., for his caddying.

The field of the 2003 U.S. Women's Open had a record number of teen golfers. Michelle was one of the fourteen who qualified. Michelle was paired with LPGA veterans Danielle Ammaccapane, age thirty-seven, and Tracy Hanson, age thirty-one. From the start of the event, Ammaccapane seemed irked at being paired with Michelle. She said little to her during their opening round.

Prior to the event, Michelle had been averaging 281 yards on her drives.

Michelle reacts to a chip onto the eigth green during the third
round of the 2003 U.S. Women's Open in North Plains, Oregon.

Her two partners were averaging around 240 yards. That created problems.

After teeing off, a golfer needs to go to their ball, pace off their yardage, and select the club for their next shot. They're not allowed to do that while their opponents are still sizing up their next shot.

One year earlier, at the LPGA Wendy's Championship, Michelle had been penalized 2 strokes for slow play. She ended up missing the cut by 2 strokes. She was determined that it wouldn't happen again.

Michelle and B. J. would begin edging their way down the fairway while their opponents were hitting their shots. That wasn't a good solution. They were moving into their opponent's line of vision which can throw off their shot. Golf etiquette mandates that a golfer and his or her caddie stand off to the side until the short hitter takes their shot.

For the first three driving holes, Ammaccapane's caddie had to keep waving Michelle and B. J. off to the side. Then there was another problem when they got to the greens. Michelle tried to speed things up by walking directly to her ball. Ammaccapane complained that Michelle was walking behind her ball to get to hers. That's known as walking "in her line" when she was trying to line up a putt.

After the round ended, Ammaccapane walked off the green before she sank her final putt. She avoided shaking hands with Michelle at the end of the opening round. Then she made scathing remarks about B. J. and Michelle to a writer from *Golf World*. "The worst was the father," Ammaccapane said. "He wouldn't get pins, couldn't rake a bunker right, kept leaving the bag in the putting line, let his player putt with the flag in. I'm trying to play in the U.S. Open and I've got Dumb and Dumber over here."

According to Michelle, Ammaccapane confronted her in the scorer's tent and told her, "You are the worst kid that I have ever seen playing golf. You will never make it playing this game. I will make money playing golf. You will not."

In Ammaccapane's version of the incident, she told *Golf Digest* she said, "Michelle, that was the worst etiquette I've ever seen. If you want to be out there, you need to do better." Ammaccapane said that she did raise her voice a little.

But David Fay, the executive director of the USGA, told *Golf Digest* that he thought that Ammaccapne's remarks were too extreme. He said that her comments, "had to do with the behavior of her father and the things that he was doing or not doing as a caddie. Would Danielle had talked like that to someone who was forty years old. Probably not, because she might have gotten a fist in her mouth."

Michelle made her feelings known by telling reporters, "I've never been so humiliated in my whole

life. . . . I can't believe that happened to me in my first Open. I think that [Danielle] should apologize. I was really surprised, because I guess I've always played with nice people."

Things calmed down a bit after B. J. admitted his mistakes and quit caddying for Michelle. "I fired myself because I caused too much trouble out there," he told *Golf Digest*. "I am new at this. I caddy for my daughter to save money. If I make mistakes out there, tell me what they are. I will learn."

Gilchrist took over as Michelle's caddie for the rest of the U.S. Women's Open. In spite of the unnerving confrontation and the publicity surrounding it, Michelle regained her composure. She finished the event by shooting two rounds of 76. That put her at 14 over par and in a tie for thirty-ninth place. She wasn't among the leaders, but it was still a stunning achievement for a thirteen-year-old girl.

In 2003, Michelle played in seven LPGA tournaments and made the cut six times. She had one top-ten finish and a scoring average of 73. She could look forward to 2004 with renewed confidence and enthusiasm.

THE LPGA AND ASIAN GOLFERS

South Korean women's golf team members Choi He-young, Chun Jae-eun, and Ru So-yeon show their gold medals at the 2006 Asian Games in Doha, Qatar.

They are talented, highly motivated, and dominating the LPGA. Who are they? Asian golfers. South Korea, in particular, has more women on the LPGA tour than any other country. And this dynamic is not expected to change anytime soon. According to the Rolex World Rankings, a ranking system for women's golf, South Korea is the country with the most players, followed by Japan and the U.S. And three of the world's Top 10 women golfers are Korean.

What accounts for the success of Korean golfers? Sports analysts say it began in 1998, when Pak Se-Ri became the first Korean woman to win the U.S. Women's Open. At the time Korea was in the midst of the Asian financial crisis, and Pak's barefoot shot to win the U.S. Open gave the country a reason to hope and created a wave of interest in the sport. In the decades that have followed Pak's win, young golfers have joined the tour as rookies, won major championships, and topped money lists. Dong-Wook Kim, executive director of the Korea Golf Association, says that in the mid-1980s Korea had fewer than two hundred junior golfers, age fifteen to eighteen, who were good enough to shoot par. Now there are about 3,000. And, Korea is not a country where you'd expect to find a lot of golfers. The country is mountainous, has only about two hundred eighteen-hole golf courses, and green fees are high, costing $150 to $200. What Korea does have going for it is competitive parents who drive their children to success. Korean parents will typically spend $3,000 to $5,000 a month to raise a champion golfer, which includes lessons, travel to tournaments, and academic tutoring. The golfers, in turn, are expected to repay the parents' investment later. Su-Jin Jang, editor of *Golf Digest Korea*, explained that the push from parents wouldn't work without the reciprocal "hyo-nyo complex," which he described as the desire to be a "good, dutiful daughter." "Hyo," or filial piety, is a virtue above all else in Confucian philosophy.

The growing presence of Asians on the tour has not been without controversy. Australian golfer Jan Stephenson told *Golf Magazine* in 2003 that "Asians are killing the (LPGA) tour. Absolutely killing it. Their lack of emotion, their refusal to speak English when they can speak English. . . . They've taken it over. If I were commissioner I would have a quota on international players that would include a quota on Asian players. I'm Australian, an international player, but I say America has to come first. Sixty percent of the tour should be American, 40 percent international."

In 2008, LPGA commissioner Carolyn Bivens did make an attempt to deal with international players by announcing that foreign players who could not conduct interviews in English would be suspended from the tour until they could. But there was such a public outcry over the perceived discriminatory policy that Bivens rescinded it and soon after resigned. ■

A view of the seventeenth hole at the Waialae
Country Club in Honolulu, Oahu, Hawaii

three
Competing Against Men

Early in 2004, Tiger Woods was asked what he thought about Michelle. He sounded like he was impressed by her achievements, but he thought that she was trying to go too far, too fast. "I think that it's pretty neat that she's playing," Woods said. "But I also look at the philosophy, too. You need to play and win, too, learn the art of winning. My dad was a big believer in that. I didn't start playing nationally until I was playing well enough to win consistently at the junior level in my own Orange County."

But by 2004 Michelle was already finished with junior golf. Her detractors might say that Michelle had only won one tournament since leaving junior golf. Her fans could answer that by saying, how many other golfers have ever won an adult tournament when they were thirteen?

The year began with Michelle competing against men in a PGA Tour event close to home. The Sony Open is held every January in Honolulu. Hawaii Governor Linda Ling made a special request to the sponsors to let Michelle be a part of the 143-player field. If Michelle made the cut, she would be the first female to qualify for a PGA Tour event since Babe Didrikson Zaharias qualified for the Tucson Open in 1945.

In the first round, Michelle shot a 2-over par 72. During that round, an estimated crowd of 3,000 people milled around to cheer her on. Many of them were wearing pins that read "Michelle No Ka Oi" (Hawaiian for "Michelle is the best"). After one round, a fourteen-year old girl was in a three-way tie with three former major champions—Jeff Sluman, Tom Lehman, and Scott Hoch.

Michelle's second round was a 2-under par 68, but that left her one stroke away from making the cut. On the par 5, 551-yard eighteenth hole, Michelle needed an eagle (2-under par) to make the cut. Her powerful tee shot traveled 299 yards before rolling to a stop. Her second shot landed on the edge of the green. Michelle's third shot landed in front of

Michelle, competing to qualify for the PGA's 2003 Sony Open, follows her tee shot on the seventeenth hole at the Pearl Country Club in Pearl Harbor, Hawaii.

the hole, but stopped rolling without dropping in. That would be the only time in 2004 that Michelle failed to make a cut. She would go on to play in seven LPGA Tour events that year.

During her attempt to qualify for the Sony Open, Michelle had a new caddie, a South African named Bobby Verwey. Verwey was a former PGA player with a genuine golfing pedigree. His father had also played on the PGA Tour and won three events. His grandfather had once won the Senior British Open. He was also a nephew of Gary Player who is widely regarded as one of the greatest players in golfing history.

From the late 1950s to the early 1970s, Player, along with Arnold Palmer and Jack Nicklaus, was regarded as one of the PGA Tour's "big three." During his lengthy career, Player won twenty-four PGA Tour events. He's also been enshrined in the World Golf Hall of Fame. In 2000, *Golf Digest* ranked Player as the eighth greatest golfer of all time.

Verwey was a longtime friend of Gary Gilchrist. In 2004, Gilchrist asked Verwey if he could caddie for Michelle. Verwey had little interest in carrying the golf bag of a fourteen-year-old girl with dreams of playing in the PGA Tour. He told Gilchrist that if he would pay his fare, he'd fly to Hawaii and see if Michelle was as great as Gilchrist claimed. As soon as he saw Michelle's powerful, fluid swing, he was ready to tote her bag. "It was the greatest thing

I had ever seen," Verwey said. "I can't put it into words. Perfection."

Verwey expected his role as Michelle's caddie to be identical to caddying for his uncle. He would gauge the wind and help her read the greens for her putting. He had already helped her putting with a tip from his uncle—keep your head still and focus on a single dimple on the ball. Then keep your eye on that spot after the ball starts rolling. But almost from the start, there was tension between him and B. J.

During the Safeway International, he advised Michelle to be aggressive with her putts instead of playing it safe. B. J. didn't like that new style. When B. J. questioned his judgment, Verwey wondered how he could caddie for Gary Player but he couldn't caddie for a fourteen-year-old girl. Finally, he told B. J., "If you want to caddy, here's the bag."

B. J. and Michelle got Verway to stay on, but he left after she ignored his advice in a crucial situation. On the par-5 eighteenth hole in the final round, he advised Michelle to tee off with a driver and go for a distance shot. She told him that B. J. told her to play it safe with a shorter shot using a 5-wood. Michelle's tee shot went into the bunker, and she finished in a tie for nineteenth, 4 strokes behind the winner, Annika Sorenstam.

In July 2004, Michelle was allowed to compete again in the U.S. Women's Open. There was

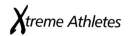

grumbling from her critics that she hadn't earned her spot. It was seen as a ploy to hype interest in the event. The USGA officials pointed out that the top thirty-five earners on the LPGA Tour money list get a slot to compete in the Open. If Michelle had been a pro in 2003, she would have been twenty-eighth on the list. Still, there were complaints that she was receiving special treatment.

In *Golf World*, Ron Sirak wrote, "Just because she is a special young player is no reason she should get special treatment. Furthermore, it is not a reason that the rules and spirit of the game should be violated. Let's reward achievement, not potential."

Michelle silenced her critics in her usual manner, by playing consistently well. She had rounds of 71-70-71-73 to finish in thirteenth place. She ended the year by making the cut seven times in seven attempts. If she had been a professional, she would have won more than $253,000. Already, B. J. was publicly rethinking his earlier statements that his daughter was still too young to turn pro. He told a writer from *ESPN The Magazine*, "At first I thought there was no chance Michelle would turn professional before graduating from Stanford. But a second alternative is going to college and then playing for a men's team. The NCAA doesn't prohibit that. Or she could play for the girl's college team. . . . If she plays for money, she might not enjoy it. Now she doesn't have to worry about making money."

While B. J. was saying that Michelle didn't have to worry about making money, her playing as an amateur golfer was costing the Wies a lot of money. Traveling to tournaments and LPGA events entailed spending money for airfare for three, van rentals, tournament fees, food, and lodging. According to golf writer Eric Adelson, from 2001 to 2003, the Wies spent more than $220,000 for Michelle's golfing expenses. Yet, B. J. kept saying that Michelle wouldn't turn pro before her eighteenth birthday

In 2004, Michelle began working with Gilchrist's former employer, David Leadbetter. Leadbetter worked at breaking down and analyzing every

Michelle with David Leadbetter during a practice round of the U.S. Women's Golf Open at the Orchards in South Hadley, Massachusetts, in 2004

component of Michelle's powerful swing. He also had Michelle meet with a sports psychologist. That may have been his way to determine if she had the mental toughness to become a full-time pro in the near future.

Michelle met with sports psychologist Jim Loehr. Loehr had co-authored a bestselling book, *The Power of Full Engagement*. Among other things, the book emphasized that ordinary people, as well as pro athletes, needed to spend time recovering from stressful activities. Some of Loehr's other clients were tennis star Monica Seles, champion boxer Ray Mancini, and hockey star Eric Lindros.

Loehr opened their first session by asking Michelle, "Why does golf mean so much to you?" Her answer stunned him. "I guess I play golf," Michelle said, "because I want to be a living testimony. Most barriers to women are self-imposed."

Loehr hardly expected someone so young to have that much self-assurance and those kinds of insights.

B. J. and Bo Wie during a practice round of the PGA 2005 Sony Open in Hawaii

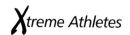

He wondered if she had somehow been coached on what to say. He then asked Michelle, "Where did you get that?" Michelle may have thought he was insinuating that she was quoting someone else. "All I've done is break records," she told him. "I started out on a boy's baseball team. I was the best hitter. Limitations are pretty artificial. I can be a statement for that."

Loehr later told a reporter, "Emotionally and mentally, she learns very fast. She has an extraordinary ability to listen and to absorb. Her optimism and resiliency are amazing. She is a gentle soul who is able to see beyond herself."

After that session, Michelle continued to stay in contact with Loehr. He was even able to help her with her schoolwork. In spite of her obvious intelligence, Michelle had a phobia about math tests. Loehr helped Michelle to conquer that, and her test scores improved.

In 2005, Michelle got off to a rocky start. She started off by playing in the PGA's Sony Open in January. One year earlier, she had missed making the cut there by only 1 stroke. But the opening round, she shot a 4-over 75. It was a harsh reminder that playing championship golf requires a high level of consistency. "After missing the cut by one last year, I think I took for granted that I was going to play better," Michelle said. "Last year everything went too easily."

The next day was even worse. Michelle shot an 80 for a two-day score of 151. She ended up missing the cut by 7 strokes. Yet, she managed to stay upbeat about how things went. "I learned a lot of things this week," Michelle said, "more than last year, I think. I think that when you play bad, you learn a lot more."

In July Michelle played in another PGA Tour even—the John Deere Classic. Once again, she was harshly criticized for competing against men. Mark Hensby, who was the event's defending champion, was particularly critical of Michelle and her parents for participation in the event. "I don't think that a fifteen-year-old girl who has done nothing at all should get a sponsor's invitation to a PGA Tour event," Hensby said. "But I don't blame the John Deere Classic or Michelle. I blame her parents and the people running her affairs. Michelle should be playing against girls her own age."

Hensby wasn't the only one criticizing Michelle and her parents. Frank Deford, a well respected writer for *Sports Illustrated*, chimed in by writing that Michelle would be better off if she would just "play against her own kind." Deford added, "You may beat most men on the golf course, but every time that you try that you're beating women's sports more than you're beating men golfers."

Michelle ignored the criticisms and shot a 1-under par in the first round of the John Deere Classic. Unfortunately, she had a double bogey (2-over par) and a bogey (1-over par) of the fourteenth and

Michelle watches along with fans as she tees off on the seventh hole with a photo of Tiger Woods looming in the background during the second round of the 2005 John Deere Classic in Silvis, Illinois.

fifteenth holes of the second round. She missed making the cut by 2 strokes.

While the critics argued about whether Michelle was helping or hurting women's golf, they couldn't deny that the John Deere Classic was benefitting from her participation. *Fortune* magazine reported that the attendance at the tournament was up 40 percent in 2005. That enabled the tournament to raise $1 million more for charity than it did in 2004.

Outside of men's events, Michelle did quite well in 2005. She played in eight tournaments and made the cut in all eight. She had three second-place finishes and one third-place finish. If she hadn't been an amateur, she would have pocketed more than $680,000 in prize money.

In 2005, the most significant event of Michelle's golf career was her attempt to qualify for the PGA's Masters Tourney. Since Michelle was still an amateur, she was allowed to compete against men in the U.S. Amateurs Public Links event. Michelle became the first female to qualify in a USGA national men's tournament.

Michelle made it into the sixty-four-player field by beating out eighty-three male amateurs. She advanced to the quarter finals before losing to Clay Ogden, who went on to win the tournament.

After hearing so much criticism that she was trying to go too far, too fast and that she was trying to

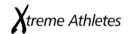

play in an area of competition where she didn't belong, Michelle publicly answered her critics. Instead of lashing out, she gave a reasoned response in an open letter to Doug Ferguson of the Associated Press. In part, it read:

> I would like to take this opportunity to clarify myself with regards to. . . not following the conventional path that many great golfers have gone through. I wanted to play in AJGA national junior golf tournaments, but I wasn't allowed to play, I was too young. By the time that I was allowed to play in the AJGA tournaments at age 13, I already made the top 10 at an LPGA major and won an adult USGA amateur tournament. I had the choice of concentrating on junior tournaments or playing the combination of professional and USGA tournaments. I chose the latter . . .
>
> People ask why I do . . . not just follow the conventional path. My answer is very simple. I always wanted to push myself to the limit. I started walking when I was 9 months old and I started reading when I was just over one year old. I started playing golf when I was

four and shot a 64 when I was 10. . . . I always wanted to do things fast. I always wanted to be the first and youngest to do things. A lot of people criticize my choice to play in the PGA Tour events but . . . it's really fun and I think that it helps me to get ready for my ultimate goal of becoming a PGA Tour member.

I am not afraid of failure and I cannot be. No matter what the critics say about me, I an going to do whatever my heart tells me to do, and I thank my parents for backing me up. Dream big and I will reach the sky; dream small and my feet will never get off the ground.

While it's believed that B. J. had a large part in writing the letter, it certainly expressed Michelle's attitudes and aspirations. There were no longer any doubts about whether Michelle would turn pro. The only question was when. It would be sooner than most people expected.

Michelle announces during a news conference in 2005 that she is turning professional. Also seated are Michael Fasulo of Sony, left, Ross Berlin of William Morris Agency, second from left, and Bob Wood of Nike, right.

four
Turning
Pro

O n October 5, 2005, Michelle formally announced that she was turning professional. She was six days away from celebrating her sixteenth birthday. Michelle wasn't old enough to get a driver's license, but she was confident that she was ready to pit herself against the best golfers in the world.

The announcement was made at a hastily arranged press conference in Honolulu. Michelle sat on a stage and looked out at the throng of reporters, photographers, and videographers and said, "I just want to thank everyone for coming today. I know that it's not that easy to come to Hawaii. And I want to thank everyone for spending this special day with me. I'm finally happy to say that I'm a pro as of today. The first time that I grabbed a golf club, I knew that I'd do it for the rest of my life and I loved it."

Then Michelle thanked two sponsors that had just made her the world's best paid female golfer:

> I'm really happy to join the Nike and Sony family, and I'm so grateful for all the opportunities they gave me, and all the flexibility they gave me. They understand that my first priority is school. I know that I'm going to graduate high school and hopefully achieve my goal of graduating college. More than ever before, I'm just going to practice harder than ever to try and become the best golfer in the world.

The lucrative endorsement deals from Nike and Sony were said to be worth $10 million a year. But when Michelle mentioned money, it was to announce that she was donating $500,000 to aid the victims of Hurricane Katrina. Katrina was the costliest storm in U.S. history. In August of 2005, it brought heavy rains and flooding to areas of Florida, Louisiana, Alabama, and Mississippi.

When Katrina hit New Orleans, it flooded about 80 percent of the city and displaced approximately 1 million people from their homes. In total, the massive storm caused more than 1,800 deaths and $125 billion in damages. "Turning pro has a lot of benefits," Michelle said. "Finally I'm so grateful to be in a position to help people. Over the last month, so many people have lost so many things, and it's really been heart wrenching. As an American citizen, I felt like it was my duty to donate $500,000 to Hurricane Katrina. Every single cent will go to the people."

A few weeks later, Michelle presented a $500,000 check for victims of Hurricane Katrina to former president Bill Clinton. After the presentation, there was a short press conference. One reporter asked Clinton, "Mr. President what does Michelle represent as an Asian-American?" Clinton replied:

> She's the future of America. Hawaii is one of only two states where the majority of the citizens are not of European heritage. That is the great gift of this country. We are held together with ideas and values. That makes it a more interesting place to be. She must be a great source of pride, pride about where we're

going. Even if other nations grow to have stronger militaries and bigger economies, we still have the power of example. She represents that.

After the press conference Michelle played a round of golf with the former president. Clinton's score went unreported, but it was reported that Michelle shot a 3-under par.

In October 2005, Michelle played in her first LPGA Tour event as a professional—the Samsung World Championship. It was a special invitation-only event where the field is limited to twenty players. There are no qualifying rounds preceding the event.

Michelle showed that she could compete with the LPGA's best. She had rounds of 70-65-71-74. That earned her a fourth-place finish and more than $53,000 in prize money. At least that's what she thought, but she was in for a very unpleasant surprise.

A few minutes after Michelle signed her final-round scorecard, a couple of rules officials approached her parents. They asked them about a drop that Michelle had taken on the seventh hole of the third round.

Michelle Wie

Michelle hits from the fairway on the sixth hole during the first round of the 2005 Samsung World Championship at Bighorn Golf Club in Palm Desert, California.

A drop is allowed when a player hits their ball into an area that is considered unplayable. The player can move their ball and drop it into an area that's playable as long as the ball isn't moved any closer to the hole.

On the seventh hole, Michelle's approach shot missed the green and landed under a bush. After making her drop, Michelle carded a par 5 for that hole. Michelle's caddie and her playing partner, Grace Park, were satisfied that Michelle hadn't moved her ball any closer to the hole. But Michael Bamberger, a writer from *Sports Illustrated*, wasn't so sure.

Bamberger stayed behind after Michelle and her party left the seventh hole. He paced off the distance from the hole to the bush. Then he paced off the distance from the drop spot to the hole. According to his measurements, her drop was one pace closer to the hole. One of golf's unique features is that there aren't any referees or umpires scrutinizing every play. The players police themselves. Michelle could have asked for a rules official to look at her drop, but she didn't think that it was necessary. Neither did

Michelle drops a ball after hitting her ball in the bushes on the seventh hole during the second round of the LPGA 2005 Samsung World Championship at Bighorn Golf Club in Palm Desert, California.

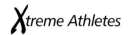

anyone else in her party. No one had objected to her drop. At least, not when it occurred.

Bamberger was really disturbed by his discovery, but he decided to wait until the next day to report it to the rules officials. By that time, Michelle had finished playing and turned in her signed scorecard. Two rules officials viewed a videotape of Michelle's drop. They thought it was inconclusive, so they asked Michelle to accompany them to the seventh hole.

Michelle and her caddie showed the officials where they thought her ball was before and after the drop. The officials paced off the distances. After pacing them off, they were still unsure if the ball had been moved closer to the hole. Then they used a measuring string to compare the two distances.

Now they were sure. Michelle had inadvertently moved her ball about one foot closer to the hole. That put her in violation of Rule 28. That violation was a 2-stroke penalty. In addition to Rule 28, Michelle had also violated Rule 6-6 which said: "The competitor is responsible for the correctness of the score recorded for each hole on his scorecard. If he returns a score for any hole lower than actually taken, he is disqualified."

According to the rules, Michelle should have recorded a 7 for that hole instead of the 5 she put on her signed scorecard. Therefore, she was disqualified and she had to forfeit her prize money. If that wasn't bad enough, Michelle also had to face the media and answer questions about her rules violations and disqualification. If she dodged the media or said "no comment," it would look like she had something to hide. She went to the media tent and explained her actions and thought process, "It was all guesswork where the ball was yesterday, where the ball was originally in the bushes . . . I'm pretty sad but, you know I think I'm going to get over it. I learned a lot from it. It's obviously not the way I wanted to begin but you know, it's all right."

While Michelle took responsibility for her actions, Bamberger received most of the blame for her disqualification. One of the most scathing criticisms came from *Washington Post* sportswriter, Leonard Shapiro:

> Back in Journalism 101, among the first principles ever driven into our young and fertile minds was the concept that reporters should never become part of the story. We're there to report and write about what we witnessed, but not inject ourselves into the action or contribute to altering the basic facts of what we've just seen or heard. But affecting the outcome of a golf tournament because you believe that a rules violation has taken place goes way above and beyond the role of the sports press . . . He was out of line. Period and end of story.

Both *Sports Illustrated* and Bamberger said that it had been the right thing to do. Bamberger defended his actions by saying, "Adherence to the rules is the underlying value of the game. To stand in silence when you see an infraction is an infraction itself." Yet, he acknowledged that he could have done it differently. "In hindsight," he said during an interview, "if I could do anything over again, I would try to intercept her between the eighteenth green and her signing the scorecard. I wish I would have done that."

Any negative publicity Michelle received from the disqualification did nothing to diminish her popularity. That was especially true in Asia. In November 2005, she was invited to compete in the Casio World Open in Japan. Even if she failed to make the cut, Michelle would receive a $1.5 million appearance fee. The tournament also gave her another opportunity to compete against men.

The event had long attracted a strong international field of golfers, because it was held after the PGA and European Tours had ended. It was also popular for its generous appearance fees and exotic location. In recent years it's been held on the Japanese island of Shikoko.

Michelle and her parents traveled to Shikoko in Casio's private jet. A small crowd of around 175 people were waiting for the Wies when they arrived at the tiny airport. Michelle delighted them by making a brief speech in Japanese. It was a subject that she had studied at the Punahou School. By the end of the week Michelle had received six offers of commercial endorsement deals from various Asian companies.

Michelle's performance at the Casio World Open revealed a major weakness in her overall game—her putting. As usual, her drives were long and straight. Her iron shots kept the ball out of sand traps, rough, and other hazards. She didn't make any bad approach shots. But a succession of missed putts caused her to miss the cut by 1 stroke.

Michelle had certainly played well, but just playing well has never been her goal. Because of her exceptional talent, she had exceptional expectations. Her failure to make the cut was a huge disappointment. She summed it up by noting, "I don't know if it proves anything that I almost made the cut."

As 2005 ended, Michelle had a lot to be proud of. Before turning pro, she had played in eight tournaments. She had three second-place finishes and one third. Her scoring average was a career-low 70.76. But to Michelle, the bottom line was that since turning pro she had one disqualification and one missed cut. She was determined that things would be better in 2006.

Michelle Wie and Kia Soul

If you haven't seen Michelle Wie's Kia commercial on television, it's readily accessible on YouTube. The thirty-two-second ad, "The Arrival," shows Michelle stirring up things at a staid country club.

Michelle watches her tee shot on the seventeenth hole during the first round of the 2005 Casio World Open golf tournament on the Japanese men's tour at Kuroshio Country Club in Kochi, Japan.

The commercial opens with some male golfers becoming transfixed at the sight of Michelle pulling up in front of a clubhouse in a flashy red 2011 Kia Soul. Even with the windows rolled up, the sounds of the song "Pro Nails," by hip-hop artist Kid Sister, can be heard blaring from within the car. ("Shake it up, up rock ya body / Make it knock, knock when you partyin' / Take a break, break in the audience / Do ya footwork break and stop again.")

The six-foot one-inch Michelle, dressed in black with a hot pink belt and golf shoes, steps out of the car and says "Morning, Boys." She then struts to the fairway and launches a soaring shot off the tee with her powerful, fluid swing.

Once Michelle launches her shot, everyone stops what they're doing. A scuba diver scrounging for golf balls in a water hazard stops to look toward the sky, a golf cart rear ends the cart in front of it, one man drops his jaw and his drink, and the other male golfers are dumbfounded by the power and distance of Michelle's drive. The ad ends with the message: "Kia Soul + Michelle Wie . . . a new way to roll."

The commercial debuted in September 2010 and aired on several networks, including the Golf Channel, ABC Family, Bravo, Oxygen, and VH1.

Apparently, Michelle has taken some kidding from some friends over the ad. "I can't ever live that down," she told Ann Miller of the *Honolulu Star-Advertiser*. ∎

Michelle chips onto the third green of Waialae Country Club
during the 2006 Sony Open golf tournament in Oahu, Hawaii.

five

Controversy and Accusations

I n 2006, Michelle made yet another attempt to make the cut in a PGA Tour event. This time it was the Sony Open in her native Hawaii. An increasingly growing number of people were getting tired of reading stories about her vying to compete with the men. The novelty had worn off. Also, since turning pro, Michelle hadn't been able to win an event on the LPGA Tour.

When asked about Michelle, most golfers on the PGA Tour would diplomatically say things like she helps attendance or she builds interest in a tournament. But by 2006, some were openly saying that a teenager who can't beat the best women golfers,

shouldn't be playing against men. Chris DiMarco, a winner of three PGA events, said, "She's a tremendous talent. . . . But I'd like to see her beat the girls her own age, and win on the LPGA Tour."

Fred Funk, an eight-time winner of PGA events, was much harsher, "Nobody belongs who doesn't qualify. You go to Q-School or earn enough to get a card. Does she belong? Absolutely not. My advice is to be the best woman out there. If you are, then come out here. She is a great role model, a great marketing tool, but she hasn't earned her way."

Since Michelle had a lucrative endorsement deal with Sony, they were eager to give her a sponsor's exemption. PGA officials also admitted that Michelle's presence would hype interest in the tournament. "We're in the entertainment business, it's more than just a golf tournament," said PGA Tour vice president Ric Clarson. "So when a player like Michelle plays in the Sony Open, it creates national and international attention on 'Can she do it?' Now that she's turned professional, there's even more attention on her progress as a player."

Once again, poor putting plagued Michelle. In her first round she shot a 9-over par 79. One golf writer blamed Michelle's putting problems on her failure to listen to her caddie, Greg Johnston. Johnston had been a caddie for LPGA star Julie Inkster before he started working for the Wies. When he was Inkster's caddie, Julie had won thirty LPGA tournaments.

Instead of relying on Johnston, Michelle used a notebook created by B. J. "We decided that Michelle cannot depend on her caddie," B. J. later explained. "We're not going to have the caddie help her read greens. She will never become a great player if she doesn't learn from her mistakes."

In the second round, Michelle improved to a 2-under par 68, but she still had five bogeys. Most of those were the result of poor putting. She missed the cut by 4 strokes. Her recurring inability to read greens and make putts was chipping away at Michelle's confidence. "You kind of start doubting yourself," Michelle admitted. "You think that it's going to break one way, then it breaks another way."

Michelle continued to generate controversy even when she didn't do anything to bring it on. In February 2006, the Rolex World Ranking came out for the first time. It was a ranking of the best pro women golfers from the five major tours they compete in. Along with the LPGA Tour it includes professional golf tours and organizations from Japan, Australia, and Korea.

Michelle made the headlines because she was ranked third even though she hadn't made any money on the LPGA Tour in 2005. She was only a fraction of a point behind Paula Creamer who had won more than $1.5 million on the LPGA Tour in 2005.

The rules for the rankings stated: "players who have not yet been included in the Rolex Rankings may be included after having played in eight eligible events over a 52-week period."

That was the exact number of LPGA Tour events that Michelle was allowed to enter as a nonmember of the LPGA. There were accusations that the rules had been rigged so Michelle would be included. Michelle answered the charges by reminding everyone that she had absolutely no input into the rankings

Michelle and her caddie, Greg Johnston, look over the eighth fairway during the final round of the 2006 LPGA Championship at the Bulle Rock Golf Course in Havre de Grace, Maryland.

rules. "It's not like I invented them," she told a group of reporters. "It's not like I woke up one day and said, 'Okay, why don't I be number three in the world?' All I did was play golf."

The one incident that generated the most controversy in 2006 was the unexpected firing of her caddie, Greg Johnston. Johnston had started caddying for Michelle at the Samsung World Championship in October 2005. It had been a difficult job. Johnston had to tolerate B. J.'s meddling and endure reading stories from various golf writers that he was responsible for her struggles.

After Michelle finished in a tie for twenty-sixth place at the Women's British Open in August 2006, Johnston was fired. Johnston learned of his firing when he got a cell phone call from Michelle's agent, Ross Berlin. In pro golf, a caddie being fired is usually a commonplace event. But usually, the golfer he caddies for will tell them in person. "I was shocked and surprised, I thought that we had a successful year," Johnston told *Golf Digest*. "And I was extremely disappointed that no one named Wie gave me the news." In a prepared

statement, Berlin said that Johnston's, "departure comes as part of Michelle's maturation as a golfer, part of which is learning from many different bright golf minds."

There was speculation that B. J. had Johnston fired because he wanted another caddie with PGA Tour experience. While Michelle had done well on the LPGA courses, she had struggled on the PGA courses with their faster greens. Whatever the reason, Johnston's sudden dismissal was a public relations disaster for the Wies. He was fired by proxy without Michelle or B. J. thanking him for his services or acknowledging his contributions. They were seen as coldhearted and impatient.

The Web site SI.com ran a poll which asked: "Are Michelle Wie's parents making a mistake with the way they're handling her career?" The two choices were: NO: She's still a teenager, and YES: She's turning into a spoiled child. There were more than 17,000 responses and more than 15,000 (89 percent) said yes.

Probably the highlight of Michelle's first full year as a pro was finally making the cut in a men's event. After seven failed attempts, Michelle qualified for the SK Telecom Open, an event on the Asian Tour. In a rain shortened fifty-four-hole tournament, Michelle finished in a tie for thirty-fifth. Even though a high school girl became only the third female to make the cut in a men's professional golf tournament, that did nothing to silence her critics. Some of them belittled the historic achievement because it wasn't a PGA Tour event.

Michelle made three other attempts in 2006 to qualify for men's tournaments. She failed in all three of them. However, she fared much better in LPGA Tour events that year. She made the cut in all eight LPGA tournaments she entered. She had one second-place finish and three third-place finishes.

Altogether, Michelle was among the top ten in six of the eight tournaments. She won more than $730,000 in prize money and had a scoring average of 70.68 on the LPGA Tour. Her critics could still argue if she deserved a number three Rolex Ranking. But when golf fans talked about the best current golfers on the LPGA Tour, Michelle Wie's name had to be included in the conversation. The Wies hoped that Michelle's success in 2006 would give her pro career some momentum in 2007. But instead of continued success, the year would be marred by a wrist injury, four missed cuts, two withdrawals from tournaments, recurring putting problems, and a steep drop in prize money and her popularity.

The last tournament Michelle had played in 2006 was the Casio World Open. It was a men's event in the Japan Golf Tour. She played badly. Michelle had rounds of 81 and 80, and she missed the cut by a whopping 17 strokes. Her parents were very concerned by her poor showing. They had a therapist take a look at her

right wrist. The diagnosis was that she had a serious injury that was causing her intense pain every time she swung a golf club.

Michelle's first appearance in a 2007 tournament was at the PGA's Sony Open in January. She had her right wrist bandaged and claimed that it was just a minor injury. But the so-called minor injury seemed to be causing major problems. Michelle had rounds of 78 and 76 and missed the cut by fourteen strokes. In early February 2007, the public relations firm representing Michelle issued a statement saying that Michelle suffered a wrist injury when she accidentally fell when running. The statement said that her wrist had been set in a hard cast and that it would take four to six weeks for her to recover.

The statement raised more questions than it answered. Where did it happen? Which wrist was it? Who is treating her? Is the injury a sprain or a fracture? Michelle's trainer, Paul Gagne, would only say that Michelle had experienced problems with both wrists over the past three years.

Instead of the four to six weeks cited in the statement, Michelle did not compete in a tournament for more than four and-a-half months. In late May she tried to qualify for the LPGA's Ginn Tribute Tournament. It's a charity event hosted by LPGA star Annika Sorenstam.

Michelle had a terrible first round. Maybe it was due to the wrist injury and the long layoff.

Michelle Wie

A man carrying a scoreboard follows Michelle, left, walking with her father and caddie, B. J. Wie, down the fairway toward the eleventh green of Waialae Country Club during the first round of the 2007 Sony Open PGA Tour golf event in Honolulu.

After twelve holes, Michelle was 12-over par. That's when the LPGA officials began discussing a little known and seldom used rule known as the "Rule of 88." The rule states that a LPGA nonmember who shoots an 88 must withdraw. After they withdraw, they're banned from competing in any other LPGA sponsored events for the rest of that calendar year.

After playing sixteen holes, Michelle had a 78. She suddenly withdrew from the tournament. Then she went to the media tent and told the reporters, "It (her wrist) felt good when I was practicing, but I kind of tweaked it in the middle of the round a little bit. So I'm just taking cautionary measures, and I know what to work on. The only way to go from here is up, so I'm feeling pretty good about it."

Michelle's explanation and the timing of her withdrawal raised a lot of doubts. Alanda Sharp, who had been playing alongside Michelle, expressed her skepticism. "She wasn't holding her wrist," Sharp said. "I think that she just had a bad day. If it was her wrist, why wait until the last two holes to withdraw?"

The skepticism increased when Michelle was seen practicing for the LPGA Championship just two days after withdrawing from the Ginn Tribute Tournament. Because of her LPGA nonmember status Michelle was allowed access to the course before the LPGA members. Now she was being seen as someone who skirted the rules (using an injury to dodge the Rule of 88) and as someone who exploited the rules (practicing before her competitors were allowed on the course).

Annika Sorenstam had never been known for being outspoken. She had hosted the Ginn Tribute Tournament. When she was asked about Michelle's withdrawal, she didn't hold back. "I just feel that there's a little bit of lack of respect and class just to kind of leave a tournament like that and then come out and practice here . . . I don't know the situation, if it's injury or whatever it is. It just seemed really weird . . . I know what it's like to be injured, I wasn't able to touch golf clubs for weeks. It's a little funny. That you pull out with an injury and then you start grinding."

When asked if Michelle withdrew because of the Rule of 88 or because of an injury, Sorenstam said, "I have no idea what it is, but I know that . . . when you get a sponsor invitation, I think that you have some responsibilities to the sponsor, to the organizer, and I can tell you that from being part of it now, it's a different side from that aspect."

The LPGA championship was yet another lackluster and forgettable outing for Michelle. She finished last in a field of 84. Michelle was the only player to have more than 300 strokes in the seventy-two-hole event. Michelle followed that up by shooting an 82 in the opening round of the U.S. Women's Open. Citing wrist pain, she withdrew after the first round.

Michelle closed out the year by missing the cut in three of five events. Her best performance of 2007 was a nineteenth-place finish in a field of twenty at the Samsung World Championship.

In 2007, Michelle earned just slightly more than $23,000 in prize money and her scoring average soared to 76.68. Still, Michelle's sponsors hadn't given up on her. In December 2007 *Forbes* magazine reported that she earned more than $19 million in commercial endorsements. ESPN golf writer Gene Wojiechowski called Michelle's horrendous season one of the year's ten biggest golf stories. He wrote:

> Teenage phenom Michelle Wie ventures dangerously close to cautionary tale as she becomes embroiled in

controversies galore. She deals with a wrist injury, is criticized by such LPGA legends as Annika Sorenstam, and plays lousy golf. Her first round withdrawal from the Ginn Tribute (hosted by Sorenstam) after 16 holes raises questions about the severity of her injury and whether she quit because she was 14 over par at the time and in danger of being barred from playing in any more 2007 LPGA events.

After her controversial withdrawal from the Ginn Tribute Tournament, Michelle had said, "the only way to go is up." But at the end of 2007, that wasn't looking very likely.

Michelle (yellow shirt) rides in the second cart with her mother Bo after she withdrew from play during the first round of the 2007 LPGA Ginn Tribute golf tournament at Rivertowne Country Club in Mount Pleasant, South Carolina.

Michelle Wie at the LPGA Championship held at Bulle Rock Golf Course in June 2009 in Havre de Grace, Maryland

SIX

Striving to Become the Best

The new year of 2008 began with Michelle competing at the Fields Open in February. Normally, she would have started the year off by playing in the Sony Open in January. That event was held in Hawaii, and it gave her home state fan base a chance to see her play.

For the past four years, Sony had given Michelle a sponsor's exemption, but things were different now. She was no longer the hot commodity and fan draw that she had once been. Her performance at the Fields Open was a continuation of her poor play.

Michelle finished in a tie for seventy-second place. That meant that seventy golfers carded a lower score than hers.

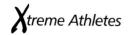

The downward spiral continued when Michelle failed to make the cut at the Michelob Ultra Open. She also failed to qualify in two later LPGA Tour events. Then at the State Farm Classic in July 2008, Michelle looked like she had finally broken out of her prolonged slump. After three rounds she was 17-under par and only 1 stroke off the lead. But, she had neglected to sign her second round scorecard. That resulted in a disqualification.

Michelle's best performance in 2008 was a sixth-place finish at the Ladies German Open which wasn't an LPGA Tour event. Her best showing in an LPGA Tour Event was a tie for twelfth place at the Canadian Women's Open. In her attempt to qualify for a PGA tournament, Michelle missed the cut by 9 strokes. Although her prize money ($62,763) and her scoring average (72.15) were significantly better than her 2007 totals, 2008 was another mediocre year in Michelle's pro career.

In 2003, golfing legend Arnold Palmer predicted that Michelle was going "to influence the golfing scene as much as Tiger, maybe more?" Now, Palmer and everyone else who had believed that Michelle was destined for greatness wondered how and why she had fallen so far, so fast. Some of the explanations were that she had tried to do too much, her putting kept getting worse, she lost her swing, and her parents had been too controlling.

Most pro golfers aren't full-time students and teenagers. Michelle turned pro while she was still a full-time student at the Punahou School. After enrolling at Stanford in September 2007, Michelle did cut back on her class load. She only took classes during the fall and winter quarters. From mid-March to late August, she was able to devote all her time to golf.

Along with the demands of school, Michelle was making frequent commercial appearances. Even for an overachiever like Michelle, that was probably too much to do when you're competing against the best pro golfers in the world. Her game suffered because she had too many commitments.

Quickly skipping from women's to men's events where the greens greatly differ, made it harder for Michelle to putt well. Putting doesn't come easily even for experienced pros. It's even harder when you're a teenager competing against adult professionals.

The powerful swing that had sent the ball rocketing off the tee and flying down the middle of the fairway began disappearing in 2006. It might have been the result of wrist injuries. It might have been from too much tinkering by her coaches. It might have been from her parents who were always hovering nearby. Whatever the reason, it was gone, and Michelle had to work to regain it.

Perhaps if Wie's parents had let Michelle have more downtime and more reliance on professional

Michelle during the
final round of LPGA
Qualifying School on
the Champions Course
at LPGA International in
Daytona Beach, Florida,
in 2008

coaching, she would have been more focused and less stressed. But B. J. and Bo had believed that under their guidance they could teach Michelle how to read greens, how to compete in both the LPGA and PGA Tours, and even how to recover from injuries. A succession of missed cuts and mediocre scores had made it much harder for Michelle to participate in pro tournaments. And the PGA had tired of her failed attempts to qualify for their tour events. The sponsor's exemptions and invitations had dried up. The LPGA had become more reluctant to allow her to compete without qualifying.

Michelle was forced to revive her career via the traditional method— by going to qualifying school and earning an LPGA Tour card. In September 2008, she took the first step by entering the LPGA Sectional Qualifying Tournament in Rancho Mirage, California. After shooting a 2-under par 70 in the opening round, Michelle refused to talk to any reporters. Through her agent, she announced that she wouldn't do any interviews before the end of the tournament.

Michelle avoided any media distractions so she could practice her putting. In the opening round she had three-putted on the sixteenth hole and missed a two-foot putt on the seventeenth hole. By shooting a 65-74-71 in the final three rounds, Michelle finished in a tie for fourth and moved on to the Final Qualifying Tournament at Daytona Beach, Florida.

Observers noted that Michelle played a more cautious game in the Final Qualifying Tournament. She was no longer trying to reach the green in 2 strokes on a par 5 hole. In five rounds she carded scores of 69-65-72-68-74. That averaged out to a very respectable 69.6 average. She finished in a tie for seventh place. That was good enough to earn her the coveted card.

Four years and two months after turning pro, Michelle was now a full fledged member of the LPGA Tour. She no longer had to worry and fret about no longer receiving invitations or sponsor's exemptions. While savoring her success, Michelle spoke candidly about the problems she had faced and the obstacles that she had overcome:

> Getting my card is a big triumph for me. I'm really proud of myself. There were times in the past couple of years, with all the injuries and stress, when I was so tired all the time . . . All I wanted to do was sleep. Even before I broke my wrist in early 2007, my whole right side was really hurting from when I hit a cart path on my downswing in my first year as a pro. I would compensate with my shoulder, neck, everything. One thing led to another and it affected my whole swing. Then I fell

while working out, and I didn't tell my
parents. . . . But then I saw that my wrist
was twisted in a weird way. The more I
moved it, the more it hurt. . . . Turns out
that I broke three bones. I was in a pre-
tend world. I didn't want to face reality.
I wanted to act like everything was okay.
The more I played, the more it hurt. The
worse I played, the more I tried to practice. It was a never-ending cycle . . . And
yes, I do want to play against men again.
Definitely. It's always been my dream,
and I'm not giving it up. But for now, I
just want to be the number one woman
golfer in the world.

Michelle didn't waste any time in taking advantage of her new opportunities. She played in nineteen
tournaments in 2009. Michelle had one win and eight
Top 10 finishes while earning more than $918,000 in
prize money.

Michelle made her debut as a member of the
LPGA Tour in her native Hawaii at the SBS Open in
mid-February. She carded rounds of 66-70-73 in the
fifty-four-hole event and finished 3 strokes behind
the winner, Angela Stanford. With eigth holes to
play, Michelle was enjoying a 3-stroke lead. A double bogey on the eleventh hole allowed Stanford to

tie Michelle. Until that point, Stanford had doubts about catching Michelle. "I didn't think she was going to make a mistake," Stanford said. "She did a lot of things smart for 10 holes. She's going to be around here for a long time."

Winning her first LPGA Tour event after earning her card would have made a strong statement that Michelle was ready to dominate the LPGA Tour. She readily acknowledged her disappointment, but she didn't dwell on it. "It's a good start to the year, I guess," Michelle said. "It's disappointing. It's not what I wanted. At the same time I had a good week. I had a good run. I take a lot of positive aspects out of the week."

In late April 2009, Michelle had a tenth-place finish at the Corona Championship in Morelia, Mexico. That was her second Top 10 finish since earning her card. Three weeks later, she enjoyed a third-place finish at the Sybase Classic. Then in late June and early July, Michelle had back-to-back Top 10 finishes at the Wegmans LPGA (tenth) and the Jamie Farr Classic (third). At Wegman's, three of Michelle's four rounds were in the 60s. At the Jamie Farr Classic all four of her rounds were under par. Over those two events, Michelle had carded a below par score in seven of eight rounds.

Michelle's last LPGA Tour event of 2009 was her first win. Rounds of 70-66-70-69 tallied up to a

13-under total of 275 at the Lorena Ochoa. Her critics could no longer say, "sure she's good, but she hasn't won anything." *Sports Illustrated* writer Alan Shipnuck explained what it meant to Michelle, her fans and the LPGA:

> The Michelle Wie era has, at long last begun. After years of injury and controversy, too much hype and money and not enough birdies, Wie won her first pro tournament Sunday afternoon. . . . Along the way Wie displayed both her awesome talent and her enduring star power, reminding everyone of what all the fuss was about in the first place. It was a deeply personal triumph, capping a period of tremendous maturation on and off the golf course.

It would be nearly a year before Michelle would have another win on the LPGA Tour. Her second victory came at the Canadian Women's Open in August 2010. After shooting an opening round 65, Michelle sealed the win with a 2-under par 70 in the final round. Her second win in less than a year showed a great improvement in her short game. "I made a lot of crucial putts today," Michelle said.

So far, in 2011 Michelle has been playing some of the best golf of her career. In four LPGA Tour

events she's had three Top 10 finishes and has a scoring average of 71.44 in sixteen rounds. Ten of the sixteen rounds have been under par and five of the under par rounds have been in the 60s.

Even if she doesn't become a dominant LPGA player like Mickey Wright, Nancy Lopez, Kathy Whitworth, or Annika Sorenstam, Michelle still plans to compete with men. Even if she becomes the world's best woman golfer, there's still the goal of becoming the best golfer in the world, period.

Michelle once pointed out, "It's the PGA Tour," she said emphatically. "Not the MPGA. I don't think it's insulting or degrading anyone by stating my goals. I have different ways of doing things."

Michelle celebrates with her parents after winning the Lorena Ochoa Invitational LPGA golf tournament in Guadalajara, Mexico, in 2009.

Timeline

1989 Born in Honolulu, Hawaii, on October 11.

1993 Begins playing golf at the age of four.

2000 Becomes the youngest player to qualify for a USGA amateur tournament.

2001 Wins the Hawaii State Junior Golf Association's Tournament of Champions; competes against men for the first time at the Manoa Cup Hawaii Amateur Match-Play Championship; at age eleven, becomes youngest player and first female to qualify for the tournament.

2002 Qualifies for her first LPGA event; plays in the Women's Division of the Hawaii State Open and wins the event by thirteen strokes.

2003 Makes the cut on an LPGA event for the first time at the Kraft Nabisco Championship; shoots a 66 in the third round. That ties her for the lowest score made by an amateur in a major tournament.

2004 Plays in her first PGA Tour event, the Sony Open; shoots 72-68 (even par) and misses cut by 1 stroke; Plays in Kraft Nabisco Championship for second time and finishes fourth.

2005 Shoots an 8-under par 280 at the McDonald's LPGA Championship and finishes in second place; plays in her third PGA event, the John Deere Open, but misses cut by 2 strokes; turns professional in October.

2006 Has third place finishes in her first two LPGA Tour events—the Fields Open and the Kraft Nabisco Championship. Fires caddie, Greg Johnston, after tying for twenty-sixth place at the Women's British Open.

2007 Begins freshman year at Stanford University; plays in seven tournaments, but only makes the cut in four of them; best outing is a nineteenth-place finish at the Samsung World Championship.

2008 Wrist injury limits her play to seven events; makes the cut in five of them; best performance is a tie for twelfth place at the Canadian Women's Open; passes the LPGA Qualifying School and becomes eligible to play full time in the 2009 LPGA Tour.

2009 Makes the cut in seventeen of nineteen events; celebrates first win on the LPGA Tour at the Lorena Ochoa Invitational; has eight Top 10 finishes and a scoring average of 70.57.

2010 Plays in nineteen events and finishes ninth on money list with $888,017; has second win on the LPGA Tour at the Canadian Women's Open; has five Top 10 finishes and a scoring average of 71.34.

2011 Opens year with a second-place finish at the Honda LPGA in Thailand; shoots under par for all four rounds and finishes with a 10-under par score of 278.

Sources

Chapter One: Little Girl, Big Swing
p. 11,   "Wowwwww . . ." Ibid.
p. 14,   "Sorry . . ." Eric Adleson, *The Sure Thing: The Making and Unmaking of Golf Phenom Michelle Wie* (New York: Ballantine Books, 2009), 21.
p. 14,   "What I really . . ." Ibid., 21.
p. 15,   "She could carry . . ." Ibid., 22.
p. 16,   "What was really unusual . . ." Jennifer Mario, "Michelle Wie's First Coach: Twenty Minutes with Casey Nakama," Travelgolf.com, January 4, 2006, http://www.travelgolf.com/departments/clubhouse/michelle-wie-coach-casey-nakama-1521.htm.
p. 16,   "Competing made her . . ." Jennifer Mario, *Michelle Wie: The Making of a Champion* (New York: St. Martin's Griffin, 2006), 23.
pp. 16-17, "I just think . . ." Adelson, *The Sure Thing: The Making and Unmaking of Gold Phenom Michelle Wie,* 24.
p. 18,   "Whether you know . . ." Ibid., 25.
p. 19,   "I was very lucky . . ." Mario, *Michelle Wie: The Making of a Champion,* 29.
p. 21,   "I had lots of fun . . ." Ibid., 35-36.
p. 22,   "That's great, but . . ." Ibid., 37.
p. 22,   "I had never . . ." Adelson, *The Sure Thing: The Making and Unmaking of Gold Phenom Michelle Wie,* 33.
pp. 22-23, "I don't think winning . . ." Ibid., 33.
p. 27,   "We need one player . . ." "Sport of the Day," *St. Petersburg Times,* February 18, 2011.

Chapter Two: A Teenage Phenom
pp. 29-30, "They loved Hawaii . . ." Mario, *Michelle Wie: The Making of a Champion,* 40.
p. 30,   "Being around her parents . . ." Ibid., 42.
p. 31,   "He didn't have to . . ." Adelson, *The Sure Thing: The Making and Unmaking of Gold Phenom Michelle Wie,* 34.
p. 31,   "Paula felt like . . ." Ibid.
p. 31,   "My philosophy is to . . ." Mario, *Michelle Wie: The Making of a Champion,* 44.
p. 39,   "The worst was . . ." Ibid., 67.
p. 39,   "You are the worst . . ." Ibid.
p. 39,   "Michelle, that was . . ." Ibid., 67-68.
p. 39,   "had to do with . . ." Ibid., 68.
pp. 39-40, "I've never been so . . ." Ibid.
p. 40,   "I fired myself . . ." Ibid., 69.

p. 43,   "hyo-nyo complex . . ." Roger Yu, "Korea's Mixture of Golf and Culture Truly a World Apart," *USA Today*, December 28, 2009, http://usatoday.com/sports/golf/2009-12-28-korean-golfers_N.htm#.

p. 43,   "Asians are killing . . ." Peter Kessler, "GolfTalk: Jan Stephenson," *Golf*, November 1, 2003.

Chapter Three: Competing Against Men

p. 45,   "I think it's pretty neat . . ." Adelson, *The Sure Thing: The Making and Unmaking of Gold Phenom Michelle Wie*, 47.

p. 49,   "It was the greatest . . ." Ibid., 53.

p. 49,   "If you want to caddy . . ." Ibid., 55.

p. 50,   "Just because she is . . ." Ibid., 61.

pp. 50-51, "At first I thought . . ." Ibid., 57.

p. 52,   "Why does golf mean so much . . ." Ibid., 59.

p. 52,   "I guess I play golf . . ." Ibid.

p. 54,   "Where did you . . ." Ibid.

p. 54,   "All I've done is . . ." Ibid.

p. 54,   "Emotionally and mentally . . ." Ibid.

p. 54,   "After missing the cut . . ." Mario, *Michelle Wie: The Making of a Champion*, 90.

p. 55,   "I learned a lot . . ." Ibid., 91.

p. 55,   "I don't think a . . ." Ibid., 98.

p. 55,   "play against her own kind," Ibid., 100.

p. 55,   "You may beat most men . . ." Ibid.

pp. 58-59, "I would like to . . ." Adelson, *The Sure Thing: The Making and Unmaking of Gold Phenom Michelle Wie*, 62-64.

Chapter Four: Turning Pro

p. 62,   "I just want to thank . . ." Mario, *Michelle Wie: The Making of a Champion*, 108.

p. 62,   "I'm really happy too . . ." Ibid.

p. 63,   "Turning pro has a lot . . ." Ibid., 113.

pp. 63-64, "She's the future of . . ." Adelson, *The Sure Thing: The Making and Unmaking of Gold Phenom Michelle Wie*, 101.

p. 69,   "It was all guesswork . . ." Mario, *Michelle Wie: The Making of a Champion*, 125.

p. 69,   "Back in Journalism 101 . . ." Ibid., 126.

p. 70,   "Adherence to the rules . . ." Ibid., 127.

p. 70,   "In hindsight . . ." Ibid.

p. 71,   "I don't know if . . ." Adelson, *The Sure Thing: The Making and Unmaking of Gold Phenom Michelle Wie*, 111.

Chapter Five: Controversy and Accusations

p. 76,   "She's a tremendous talent . . ." Adelson, *The Sure Thing: The Making and Unmaking of Gold Phenom Michelle Wie,* 118.

p. 76,   "Nobody belongs who doesn't . . ." Ibid., 119.

p. 76,   "We're in the entertainment business . . ." Associated Press, "Wie to Start Against the Men at Sony Open," Thegolfchannel. com, October 26, 2005, www.golfchannel.com/tour-insider/ wie-start-2006-men-sony-open-17911/.

p. 77,   "We decided Michelle cannot . . ." Adelson, *The Sure Thing: The Making and Unmaking of Gold Phenom Michelle Wie,* 121.

p. 77,   "You kind of start . . ." Ibid., 122.

pp. 78-79, "It's not like I . . ." Ibid., 127.

p. 79,   "I was shocked . . ." Eric Matuszewski, "Michelle Wie Fires Caddie After Finishing 26 at British Open," Bloomberg.com, August 8, 2006, http://www.bloomberg.com/apps/news?pid=newsarchive&sid=awB YmwZZ5ses&refer=home.

p. 80,   "departure comes at a time . . ." Ibid.

p. 84,   "It (her wrist) felt good when . . ." Adelson, *The Sure Thing: The Making and Unmaking of Gold Phenom Michelle Wie,* 229.

p. 84,   "She wasn't holding . . ." Ibid.

p. 85,   "I just feel that . . ." Ibid. 230.

p. 85,   "I have no idea . . ." Ibid.

pp. 86-87, "Teenage phenom Michelle Wie . . ." Gerry Brown and Michael Morrison, eds., *2008 ESPN Sports Almanac* (New York: Random House, 2007), 844.

Chapter Six: Striving to Become the Best

p. 90,   "to influence the golfing scene . . ." Adelson, *The Sure Thing: The Making and Unmaking of Gold Phenom Michelle Wie,* 239.

pp. 94-95, "Getting my card is . . ." Ibid., 242-244.

p. 96,   "I didn't think she was . . ." "Michelle Wie Stumbles on Back 9, Angela Stanford Wins SBS Open," *New York Daily News,* February 14, 2009.

p. 96,   "It's a good start . . ." Ibid.

p. 97,   "The Michelle Wie era . . ." Alan Shipnuck, "After Years in Spotlight, Michelle Wie Wins First Pro Tournament," Golf.com, November 18, 2009, www.golf.com/tours_news/article/print/0,32618,1939582,00.html.

p. 97,   "I made a lot of crucial . . ." "Michelle Wie Wins Canadian Women's Open, Second LPGA Tour Title," AOLNews com, April 29, 2010, www.aolnews.com/2010/08/29/ michelle-wie-wins-canadian-womens-open-second-lpga-tour-title/.

p. 99,   "It's the PGA Tour . . ." Adelson, *The Sure Thing: The Making and Unmaking of Gold Phenom Michelle Wie,* 72-73.

Bibliography

Adelson, Eric. *The Sure Thing The Making and Unmaking of Golf Phenom Michelle Wie*. New York: ESPN Books, 2009.

Associated Press. "Wie Keeps It Simple, Advances to Round of 16." *The New York Times*, May 21, 2010.

———. "Wie Ties for Seventh With Two-over 74; Lewis Is Medalist With 3-under 69." ESPN.com. http://sports.espn.go.com/golf/news/story?id=3752292.

———. "Wie to Start 2006 Against the Men at Sony Open." Thegolfchannel.com. www.thegolfchannel.com/tour-insider/wie-start-2006-men-sony-open-17911/.

Brown, Gerry, and Michael Morrison, eds. *2008 ESPN Sports Almanac*. New York: Random House, 2007.

Ihlwan, Moon. "Virtual Reality Golf Takes Off in Korea." *Business Week*, October 27, 2008.

"International Field Set for Next Week's LPGA Sectional Qualifying Tournament." LPGA.com. www.lpga.com/content_1.aspx?pid=17192&mid=1.

Jempty, Bill. "Michelle Wie, Stacy Lewis Advance at LPGA Qualifying School." Wizbangsports.com, http://wizbangsports.com/2008/09/michelle_wie_stacy_lewis_advan.php.

Mario, Jennifer. "Michelle Wie's First Coach: Twenty Minutes with Casey Nakama." Travelgolf.com. http://www.travelgolf.com/departments/clubhouse/michelle-wie-coach-casey-nakama-1521.htm.

Matuszewski, Erik. "Michelle Wie Fires Caddie After Finishing 26th at British Open." Bloomberg.com, http://www.bloomberg.com/apps/news?pid=awBYmwZZ5ses&refer=home.

McLuskey, Des. "Michelle Wie Gets Soaked With Beer After Breakthrough." *Bloomberg News*, November 16, 2009.

"Michelle Wie." Seoulsisters.com, http://www.seoulsisters.com/players/misc/wie.htm.

"Michelle Wie Shoots 70 at LPGA Q-school Sectional." Golf.com. http://www.golf.com/golf/tours_news/article/0,28136,1841435,00.html.

Miller, Ann. "The Smile is Back for Big Wiesy." *Honolulu Star-Advertiser*, September 2, 2010.

"Quick 18 With Michelle Wie." LPGA.com. http://www.lpga.com/content_1.aspx?pid=21910&mid=2.

Shipnuck, Alan. "After Years in Spotlight, Michelle Wie Wins First Pro Tournament." *Sports Illustrated*, November 18, 2009.

Smith, Stephen W. "Golfer Michelle Wie, 15, Turns Pro." CBSNews. com. http://www.cbsnews.com/stories/2005/10/05/national/main917086.shtml.

Sobel, Jason. "Wie Shoots 13-under for First Pro Win." ESPN.com. http://sports.espn.go.com/golf/news/story?id=4657907.

"Sport of the Day." *St. Petersburg Times*, February 8, 2011.

Thompson, Edgar. "Stuck in the Fough, The LPGA Tour, With Its U.S. Foothold Shrinking, Struggles for Relevancy." *Palm Beach Post*, February 20, 2011.

"Wie Starts Season Ranked Number 9 In Rolex Ratings." LPGA.com. http://www.lpga.com/content_1.aspx?pid=23046&mid=2.

Yang, Jung A. "North Korea's Golf Course, 100 Members of the Elite." Dailynk.com. http://www.dailynk.com/english/read.php?cataId=nk01500&num=1400.

Yu, Roger. "Korea's Mixture of Golf and Culture Truly a World Apart." *USA Today*, December 28, 2009.

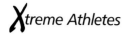

Glossary

Ace - A hole in one.

Bunker - An area of ground which has had turf or dirt removed and has been replaced with water, sand, or tall grass. It's also known as a trap.

Birdie - 1 stroke under the par for a hole.

Bogey - 1 stroke over par for a hole.

Clubhead - The base of the club where the ball is intended to be struck.

Eagle - 2 strokes under par for a hole.

Fairway - An area of closely mown grass between the tee and the green.

Handicap - A number based on a golfer's playing ability. The better the golfer, the lower the handicap.

Hook - A stroke where the ball curves to the left or right of the target. A right-handed player hooks the ball to the left and a left handed player hooks the ball to the right.

Iron - A metal golf club numbered 1-9, with a thin, flat, angled face.

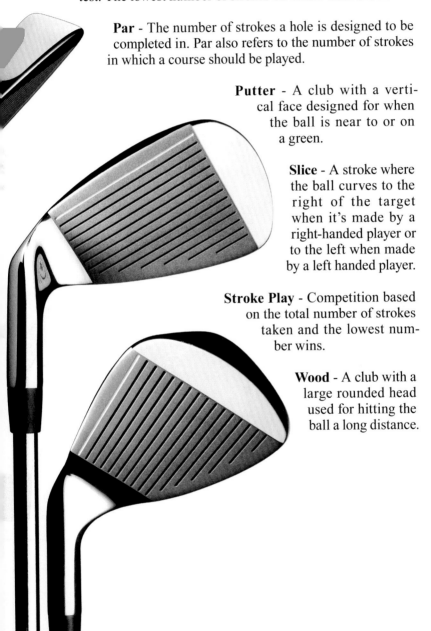

Match Play - A golf competition where each hole is a separate contest. The lowest number of strokes on a hole wins the hole.

Par - The number of strokes a hole is designed to be completed in. Par also refers to the number of strokes in which a course should be played.

Putter - A club with a vertical face designed for when the ball is near to or on a green.

Slice - A stroke where the ball curves to the right of the target when it's made by a right-handed player or to the left when made by a left handed player.

Stroke Play - Competition based on the total number of strokes taken and the lowest number wins.

Wood - A club with a large rounded head used for hitting the ball a long distance.

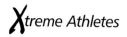

Web sites

http://www.lpga.com
Official Web site of the LPGA has photos, a biography, news stories, and statistics about Michelle Wie and all the other golfers on the LPGA Tour.

http://www.missmichellewie.com
Photos and news about Michelle along with her tournament history and links to other Web sites where she is featured.

http://www.seoulsisters.com
Biographies and photo galleries of Michelle and all the other Korean and Korean American golfers on the LPGA Tour.

http://www.thewiewatch.com
Capsule summaries of every tournament Michelle has played in going back to 2006. It's updated every time Michelle plays.

Index

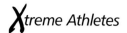

Photo Credits

Book cover and interior design by Derrick Carroll Creative.